Books by James Merrill

BRAVING THE ELEMENTS

BRAVING THE ELEMENTS

POEMS BY

JAMES MERRILL

ATHENEUM   NEW YORK

1972

These poems have appeared in the following magazines:

ANTAEUS (*Strato in Plaster*)

THE BROWN BAG (*Under Mars*)

COUNTER/MEASURES (*In Monument Valley*)

HARPER'S MAGAZINE (*Pieces of History, Willowware Cup, Syrinx*)

THE HUDSON REVIEW (*Days of 1935*)

MADRONA (*Log*)

NEW AMERICAN REVIEW (*Days of 1971, The Victor Dog*)

THE NEW YORKER (*In Nine Sleep Valley, Under Libra: Weights and Measures, Up and Down*)

THE NEW YORK REVIEW OF BOOKS (*After the Fire, 18 West 11th Street*)

PERSPECTIVE (*Electra: a Translation*)

POETRY (*Another April, Banks of a Stream Where Creatures Bathe, The Black Mesa, Komboloi, Flèche d'Or*)

SHENANDOAH (*Dreams About Clothes*)

TRANSATLANTIC REVIEW (*Mandala*)

Library of Congress catalog card number 72-78488

Published simultaneously in Canada by McClelland and Stewart Ltd

Manufactured in the United States of America by

Halliday Lithograph Corporation, West Hanover, Massachusetts

Designed by Harry Ford

First Printing August 1972

Second Printing November 1972

For my mother

Contents

BRAVING THE ELEMENTS

Log

Then when the flame forked like a sudden path
I gasped and stumbled, and was less.
Density pulsing upward, gauze of ash,
Dear light along the way to nothingness,
What could be made of you but light, and this?

After the Fire

Everything changes; nothing does. I am back,
The doorbell rings, my heart leaps out of habit,
But it is only Kleo – how thin, how old! –
Trying to smile, lips chill as the fallen dusk.

She has brought a cake "for tomorrow"
As if tomorrows were still memorable.
We sit down in the freshly-painted hall
Once used for little dinners. (The smoke cleared
On no real damage, yet I'd wanted changes,
Balcony glassed in, electric range,
And wrote to have them made after the fire.)
Now Kleo's eyes begin to stream in earnest –
Tears of joy? Ah, troubles too, I fear.
Her old mother has gone off the deep end.

From their basement window the yiayia, nearly ninety,
Hurls invective at the passing scene,
Tea bags as well, the water bill, an egg
For emphasis. A strange car stops outside?
She cackles *Here's the client! Paint your face,*
Putana! to her daughter moistening
With tears the shirt she irons. Or locks her out
On her return from watering, with tears,
My terrace garden. (I will see tomorrow
The white oleander burst from its pot in the rains.)
Nor is darling Panayioti, Kleo's son,
Immune. Our entire neighbourhood now knows
As if they hadn't years before
That he is a *Degenerate!* a *Thieving*
Faggot! just as Kleo is a *Whore!*

I press Kleo's cold hand and wonder
What could the poor yiayia have done
To deserve this terrible gift of hindsight,

4

These visions that possess her of a past
When Kleo really was a buxom armful
And "Noti" cruised the Naval Hospital,
Slim then, with teased hair. Now he must be forty,
Age at which degeneration takes
Too much of one's time and strength and money.
My eyes brim with past evenings in this hall,
Gravy-spattered cloth, candles minutely
Guttering in the love-blinded gaze.
The walls' original oldfashioned colors,
Cendre de rose, warm flaking ivory –
Colors last seen as by that lover's ghost
Stumbling downstairs wound in a sheet of flame –
Are hidden now forever but not lost
Beneath this quiet sensible light gray.

Kleo goes on. The yiayia's *warm*,
What can it mean? She who sat blanketed
In mid-July now burns all day,
Eats only sugar, having ascertained
Poison in whatever Kleo cooks.
Kill me, there'll be an autopsy,
Putana, matricide, I've seen to that!
I mention my own mother's mother's illness,
Querulous temper, lucid shame.
Kleo says weeping that it's not the same,
There's nothing wrong, according to the doctor,
Just that she's old and merciless. And warm.

Next day I visit them. Red-eyed Kleo
Lets me in. Beyond her, bedclothes disarrayed,
The little leaden oven-rosy witch
Fastens her unrecognizing glare
Onto the lightest line that I can spin.
"It's me, yiayia! Together let us plumb

Depths long dry" – getting no further, though,
Than Panayioti's anaconda arms:

"Ah Monsieur Tzim, bon zour et bon retour!
Excuse mon déshabillé. Toute la nuit
Z'ai décoré l'église pour la fête
Et fait l'amour, le prêtre et moi,
Dans une alcove derrière la Sainte Imaze.
Tiens, z'ai un cadeau pour toi,
Zoli foulard qui me va pas du tout.
Mais prends-le donc, c'est pas volé –
Ze ne suis plus voleur, seulement volaze!"

Huge, powerful, bland, he rolls his eyes and r's.
Glints of copper wreathe his porcelain brow
Like the old-time fuses here, that blow so readily.
I seem to know that crimson robe,
And on his big fat feet – my slippers, ruined.
Still, not to complicate affairs,
Remembering also the gift of thumb-sized garnet
Bruises he clasped round Aleko's throat,
I beam with gratitude. Meanwhile
Other translated objects one by one
Peep from hiding: teapot, towel, transistor.
Upon the sideboard an old me
Scissored from its glossy tavern scene –
I know that bare arm too, flung round my shoulder –
Buckles against a ruby glass ashtray.
(It strikes me now, as happily it did not
The insurance company, that P caused the fire.
Kleo's key borrowed for a rendezvous,
A cigarette left burning . . . Never mind.)
Life like the bandit Somethingopoulos
Gives to others what it takes from us.

Some of those embers can't be handled yet.

I mean to ask whose feast it is today
But the room brightens, the yiayia shrieks my name –
It's Tzimi! He's·returned!
– And with that she returns to human form,
The snuffed-out candle-ends grow tall and shine,
Dead flames encircle us, which cannot harm,
The table spread, she croons, and I
Am kneeling pressed to her old burning frame.

Pieces of History

I

Depressions visible from the air
Even today help you locate Qatum –
Huge red sandbox somewhere at whose heart
Twin-chambered lay the royal pair

How long equipped for a fantastic trek
Back to the sun and moon they had to be.
Time would have undressed them to the teeth,
Sucked their bones but spared their filigree.

I broke in with Daud. Taboos
Were for the old. Harp, harper, palanquin and groom,
The brittle ores of dagger-clasp, of wreath,
Pellmell, hers, his, theirs, ours – by evening, what was whose?

2

I was only nine when an emotional war,
The Spanish one, streaked with powder, entered our house.
What right had she to arouse me, child that I was?
Yet she tried to. Wars are whores, they have no shame.

And how about the issue of female suffrage,
Dead now, but ripe enough in her heyday to be my mother?
Thinking of her, I peek at your ballot box
And you burn with aversion. Young people are all the same.

These eyes have turned Aunt Tom into a vegetable
And my godfather into sepia and ormolu.
Old women I hardly remember come up to say my name
And kiss me. One day you will love me, even you.

3
Up from wrinkled headlands see her loom
Enlarged by emanations, white as pearl or lime.
The lone surveyor working overtime
Puts away his useless pendulum.

Dream: A letter comes from Miss Thyra Reese
Who drummed the credenda of progress into some of us
And knew by heart "The Chambered Nautilus,"
Asking what have I done with her pince-nez and teeth.

There on the moon, her meaning now one swift
Footprint, a man my age with a glass face
Empty of insight signals back through space
To the beclouded cortex which impelled his drift.

In Monument Valley

One spring twilight, during a lull in the war,
At Shoup's farm south of Troy, I last rode horseback.
Stillnesses were swarming inward from the evening star
Or outward from the buoyant sorrel mare

Who moved as if not displeased by the weight upon her.
Meadows received us, heady with unseen lilac.
Brief, polyphonic lives abounded everywhere.
With one accord we circled the small lake.

Yet here I sit among the crazy shapes things take.
Wasp-waisted to a fault by long abrasion,
The "Three Sisters" howl. "Hell's Gate" yawns wide.
I'm eating something in the cool Hertz car

When the shadow falls. There has come to my door
As to death's this creature stunted, cinder-eyed,
Tottering still half in trust, half in fear of man –
Dear god, a horse. I offer my apple-core

But she is past hunger, she lets it roll in the sand,
And I, I raise the window and drive on.
About the ancient bond between her kind and mine
Little more to speak of can be done.

Days of 1935

Ladder horned against moonlight,
Window hoisted stealthily –
Thats what I'd steel myself at night
To see, or sleep to see.

My parents were out partying,
My nurse was old and deaf and slow.
Way off in the servants' wing
Cackled a radio.

On the Lindbergh baby's small
Cold features lay a spell, a swoon.
It seemed entirely plausible
For my turn to come soon,

For a masked and crouching form
Lithe as tiger, light as moth,
To glide towards me, clap a firm
Hand across my mouth,

Then sheer imagination ride
Off with us in its old jalopy,
Trailing bedclothes like a bride
Timorous but happy.

A hundred tenuous dirt roads
Dew spangles, lead to the web's heart.
That whole pale night my captor reads
His brow's unwrinkling chart.

Dawn. A hovel in the treeless
Trembling middle of nowhere,
Hidden from the world by palace
Walls of dust and glare.

A lady out of *Silver Screen*,
Her careful rosebud chewing gum,
Seems to expect us, lets us in,
Nods her platinum

Spit curls deadpan (I will wait
Days to learn what makes her smile)
At a blue enamel plate
Of cold greens I can smell –

But swallow? Never. The man's face
Rivets me, a lightning bolt.
Lean, sallow, lantern-jawed, he lays
Pistol and cartridge belt

Between us on the oilskin (I
Will relive some things he did
Until I die, until I die)
And clears his throat: "Well, Kid,

You've figured out what's happening.
We don't mean to hurt you none
Unless we have to. Everything
Depends on, number one,

How much you're worth to your old man,
And, number two, no more of this – "
Meaning my toothprints on his hand,
Indenture of a kiss.

With which he fell upon the bed
And splendidly began to snore.
"Please, I'm sleepy too," I said.
She pointed to the floor.

The rag rug, a rainbow threadbare,
Was soft as down. For good or bad
I felt her watching from her chair
As no one ever had.

Their names were Floyd and Jean. I guess
They lived in what my parents meant
By sin: unceremoniousness
Or common discontent.

"Gimme – Wait – Hey, watch that gun –
Why don't these dumb matches work –
See you later – Yeah, have fun –
Wise guy – Floozie – Jerk – "

Or else he bragged of bygone glories,
Stores robbed, cars stolen, dolls betrayed,
Escape from two reformatories.
Said Jean, "Wish you'd of stayed."

To me they hardly spoke, just watched
Or gave directions in dumb show.
I nodded back like one bewitched
By a violent glow.

Each morning Floyd went for a ride
To post another penciled note.
Indignation nation wide
Greeted what he wrote.

Each afternoon, brought papers back.
One tabloid's whole front page was spanned
By the headline bold and black:
FIEND ASKS 200 GRAND.

13

Photographs too. My mother gloved,
Hatted, bepearled, chin deep in fur.
Dad glowering – was it true he loved
Others beside her?

Eerie, speaking likenesses.
One positively heard her mild
Voice temper some slow burn of his,
"Not before the child."

The child. That population map's
Blanknesses and dots were me!
Mine, those swarming eyes and lips,
Centers of industry

Italics under which would say
(And still do now and then, I fear)
Is This Child Alive Today?
Last Hopes Disappear.

Toy ukelele, terrorstruck
Chord, the strings so taut, so few –
Tingling I hugged my pillow. *Pluck*
Some deep nerve went. I knew

That life was fiction in disguise.
My teeth said, chattering in Morse,
"Are you a healthy wealthy wise
Red-blooded boy? Of course?

Then face the music. Stay. Outwit
Everyone. Captivity
Is beckoning – make a dash for it!
It will set you free."

Sometimes as if I were not there
He put his lips against her neck.
Her head lolled sideways, just like Claire
Coe in "Tehuantepec."

Then both would send me looks so heaped
With a lazy, scornful mirth,
This was growing up, I hoped,
The first flushed fruits of earth.

One night I woke to hear the room
Filled with crickets – no, bedsprings.
My eyes dilated in the gloom,
My ears made out things.

Jean: The kid, he's still awake . . .
Floyd: Time he learned . . . Oh baby . . . God . . .
Their prone tango, for my sake,
Grew intense and proud.

And one night – pure "Belshazzar's Feast"
When the slave-girl is found out –
She cowered, face a white blaze ("Beast!")
From his royal clout.

Mornings, though, she came and went,
Buffed her nails and plucked her brows.
What had those dark doings meant?
Less than the fresh bruise

Powdered over on her cheek.
I couldn't take my eyes away.
Let hers meet them! Let her speak!
She put down *Photoplay:*

"Do you know any stories, Kid?
Real stories – but not real, I mean.
Not just dumb things people did.
Wouldja tell one to Jean?"

I stared at her – *she* was the child! –
And a tale came back to me.
Bluebeard. At its end she smiled
Half incredulously.

I spun them out all afternoon.
Wunspontime, I said and said . . .
The smile became a dainty yawn
Rose-white and rose-red.

The little mermaid danced on knives,
The beauty slept in her thorn bower.
Who knows but that our very lives
Depend on such an hour?

The fisherman's hut became Versailles
Because he let the dolphin go . . .
Jean's lids have shut. I'm lonely. I
Am pausing on tiptoe

To marvel at the shimmer breath
Inspires along your radii,
Spider lightly running forth
To kiss the simple fly

Asleep. A chance to slip the net,
Wriggle down the dry stream bed,
Now or never! This child cannot.
An iridescent thread

Binds him to her slumber deep
Within a golden haze made plain
Precisely where his fingertip
Writes on the dusty pane

In spit his name, address, age nine
– Which the newspapers and such
Will shortly point to as a fine
Realistic touch.

Grown up, he thinks how S, T, you –
Second childhood's alphabet
Still unmastered, it is true,
Though letters come – have yet

Touched his heart, occasioned words
Not quickened by design alone,
Responses weekly winging towards
Your distance from his own,

Distance that much more complex
For its haunting ritornel:
Things happen to a child who speaks
To strangers, mark it well!

Thinks how you or V – where does
It end, will *any*one have done? –
Taking the wheel (cf. those "Days
Of 1971")

Have driven, till his mother's Grade
A controls took charge, or handsome
Provisions which his father made
Served once again as ransom,

17

Driven your captive far enough
For the swift needle on the gauge
To stitch with delicate kid stuff
His shoddy middle age.

Here was Floyd. The evening sun
Filled his eyes with funny light.
"Junior, you'll be home real soon."
To Jean, "Tomorrow night."

What was happening? Had my parents
Paid? pulled strings? Or maybe I
Had failed in manners, or appearance?
Must this be goodbye?

I'd hoped I was worth more than crime
Itself, which never paid, could pay.
Worth more than my own father's time
Or mother's negligée

Undone where dim ends barely met,
This being a Depression year . . .
I'd hoped, I guess, that they would let
Floyd and Jean keep me here.

We ate in silence. He would stop
Munching and gaze into the lamp.
She wandered out on the dark stoop.
The night turned chill and damp.

When she came in, she'd caught a bug.
She tossed alone in the iron bed.
Floyd dropped beside me on the rug;
Growled, "Sleep." I disobeyed.

Commenced a wary, mortal heat
Run neck by nose. Small fingers felt,
Sore point of all that wiry meat,
A nipple's tender fault.

Time stopped. His arm somnambulist
Had circled me, warm, salt as blood.
Mine was the future in his fist
To get at if I could,

While his heart beat like a drum
And *Oh baby* faint and hoarse
Echoed from within his dream . . .
The next day Jean was worse

– Or I was. Dawn discovered me
Sweating on my bedroom floor.
Was there no curbing fantasy
When one had a flair?

Came those nights to end the tale.
I shrank to see the money tumble,
All in 20s, from a teal
Blue Studebaker's rumble

Down a slope of starlit brush.
Sensed with anguish the foreseen
Net of G-men, heard the hush
Deepen, then Floyd's voice ("Jean,

Baby, we've been doublecrossed!")
Drowned out by punctual crossfire
That left the pillow hot and creased.
By three o'clock, by four,

They stood in handcuffs where the hunt
Was over among blood-smeared rocks
– Whom I should not again confront
Till from the witness-box

I met their stupid, speechless gaze.
How empty they appeared, how weak
By contrast with my opening phrase
As I began to speak:

"You I adored I now accuse . . ."
Would imagination dare
Follow that sentence like a fuse
Sizzling towards the Chair?

See their bodies raw and swollen
Sagging in a skein of smoke?
The floor was reeling where I'd fallen.
Even my old nurse woke

And took me in her arms. I pressed
My guilty face against the void
Warmed and scented by her breast.
Jean, I whispered, Floyd.

A rainy day. The child is bored.
While Emma bakes he sits, half-grown.
The kitchen dado is of board
Painted like board. Its grain

Shiny buff on cinnamon
Mimics the real, the finer grain.
He watches icing sugar spin
Its thread. He licks in vain

Heavenly flavors from a spoon.
Left in the metallic bowl
Is a twenty-five watt moon.
Somewhere rings a bell.

Wet walks from the East porch lead
Down levels manicured and rolled
To a small grove where pets are laid
In shallow emerald.

The den lights up. A Sazerac
Helps his father face the *Wall
Street Journal*. Jules the colored (black)
Butler guards the hall.

Tel & Tel executives,
Heads of Cellophane or Tin,
With their animated wives
Are due on the 6:10.

Upstairs in miles of spangled blue
His mother puts her make-up on.
She kisses him sweet dreams, but who –
Floyd and Jean are gone –

Who will he dream of? True to life
He's played them false. A golden haze
Past belief, past disbelief . . .
Well. Those were the days.

Mandala

*"I advise you to meditate upon
the Third Eye."* – LETTER FROM T

OK. I see a whirlpool
Yawning at the heart of things.
In grave procession seasons, elements, creatures, kings
Ride the slowly sinking carrousel

From which they will never, not in ten million
Years, nor in any form, return. They are about to merge
With Nothing mirrored as a demiurge
Vaguely Mongolian.

Outside that circus, trivia.
Everyone else must redo his clumsy exercise
Life after life. No wonder the third eye's
Lid grows heavier.

All the same, I am setting my cat
Sights on two or three
More flings here in the dark. A certain ingenuity
Goes into meriting that.

One wants, to plot the boomerang curve
That brings one back,
Beyond the proper coordinates of Have and Lack,
A flair for when to swerve

Off into utter pointlessness –
Issues that burn like babies, furrows of grief and sloth
Sown with sperm, no talent glinting forth
Except for how to dress

At those last brunches on the yacht
While the pearly trough kept pace and the Martini pitcher
Sweated and swirled, becoming second nature
– And oh yes, not

To return as a slug or a mayfly, plus one's GI pair
Shortsighted brown, wants to carry, as I do,
A peasant "eye" of blue
Glass daubed with yellow. Turkish work. So there,

Your point's made, I'm an infidel.
But who needs friends
To remind him that nothing either lasts or ends?
Garrulous as you, dear, time will tell.

18 West 11th Street

In what at least
Seemed anger the Aquarians in the basement
Had been perfecting a device

For making sense to us
If only briefly and on pain
Of incommunication ever after.

Now look who's here. Our prodigal
Sunset. Just passing through from Isfahan.
Filled by him the glass

Disorients. The swallow-flights
Go word by numbskull word
   – Rebellion . . . Pentagon . . . Black Studies –

Crashing into irreality,
Plumage and parasites
Plus who knows what of the reptilian,

Till wit turns on the artificial lights
Or heaven changes. The maid,
Silent, pale as any victim,

Comes in, identifies;
Yet brings new silver, gives rise to the joint,
The presidency's ritual eclipse.

Take. Eat. His body to our lips. The point
Was anger, brother? Love? Dear premises
Vainly exploded, vainly dwelt upon.

Item: the carpet.
Identical bouquets on black, rose-dusted
Face in fifty funeral parlors,

Scentless and shaven, wall-to-wall
Extravagance without variety . . .
That morning's buzzing vacuum be fed

By ash of metropolitan evening's
Smoker inveterate between hot bouts
Of gloating over scrollwork,

The piano (three-legged by then like a thing in a riddle)
Fingered itself provocatively. Tones
Jangling whose tuner slept, moon's camphor mist

On the parterre compounding
Chromatic muddles which the limpid trot
Flew to construe. Up from camellias

Sent them by your great-great-grandfather,
Ghosts in dwarf sateen and miniver
Flitted once more askew

Through *Les Sylphides*. The fire was dead. Each summer,
While onto white keys miles from here
Warm salt chords kept breaking, snapping the strings,

The carpet – its days numbered –
Hatched another generation
Of strong-jawed, light-besotted saboteurs.

A mastermind
Kept track above the mantel. The cold caught,
One birthday in its shallows, racked

The weak frame, glazed with sleet
Overstuffed aunt and walnut uncle. Book
You could not read. Some utterly

Longed-for present meeting other eyes'
Blue arsenal of homemade elegies,
Duds every one. The deed

Diffused. Your breakfast *Mirror* put
Late to bed, a fever
Flashing through the veins of linotype:

NIX ON PEACE BID PROPHET STONED
FIVE FEARED DEAD IN BOMBED DWELLING
– Bulletin-pocked columns, molten font

Features would rise from, nose for news
Atwitch, atchoo, God bless you!
Brought to your senses (five feared? not one bit)

Who walking home took in
The ruin. The young linden opposite
Shocked leafless. Item: the March dawn.

Shards of a blackened witness still in place.
The charred ice-sculpture garden
Beams fell upon. The cold blue searching beams.

Then all you sought
No longer, B came bearing. An arrangement
In time known simply as That June –

Fat snifter filled with morbidest
Possibly meat-eating flowers,
So hairy-stemmed, red-muscled, not to be pressed.

Pinhead notions underwater, yours,
Quicksilvered them afresh.
You let pass certain telltale prints

Left upon her in the interim
By that winter's person, where he touched her.
Still in her life now, was he, feeling the dim

Projection of your movie on his sheet?
Feeling how you reached past B towards him,
Brothers in grievance? But who grieves!

The night she left ("One day you'll understand")
You stood under the fruitless tree. The streetlight
Cast false green fires about, a tragic

Carpet of shadows of blossoms, shadows of leaves.
You understood. You would not seek rebirth
As a Dalmatian stud or Tiny Tim.

Discolorations from within, dry film
Run backwards, parching, scorching, to consume
Whatever filled you to the brim,

Fierce tongue, black
Fumes massing forth once more on
Waterstilts that fail them. The

Commissioner unswears his oath. Sea serpent
Hoses recoil, the siren drowns in choking
Wind. The crowd has thinned to a coven

Rigorously chosen from so many called. Our
Instant trance. The girl's
Appearance now among us, as foreseen

Naked, frail but fox-eyed, head to toe
(Having passed through the mirror)
Adorned with heavy shreds of ribbon

Sluggish to bleed. She stirs, she moans the name
Adam. And is *gone*. By her own
Broom swept clean, god, stop, behind this

Drunken backdrop of debris, airquake,
Flame in bloom – a pigeon's throat
Lifting, the puddle

Healed. To let:
Cream paint, brown ivy, brickflush. Eye
Of the old journalist unwavering

Through gauze. Forty-odd years gone by.
Toy blocks. Church bells. Original vacancy.
O deepening spring.

Another April

The panes flash, tremble with your ghostly passage
Through them, an x-ray sheerness billowing, and I have risen
But cannot speak, remembering only that one was meant
To rise and not to speak. Young storm, this house is yours.
Let your eye darken, your rain come, the candle reeling
Deep in what still reflects control itself and me.
Daybreak's great gray rust-veined irises humble and proud
Along your path will have laid their foreheads in the dust.

In Nine Sleep Valley

1

Trying to read in Nature's book
The pages (canyon forest landslide lake)
Turn as the road does, the stock characters
Come and (marmot mallard moose)

Go too quickly to believe in. Look,
I'm told, but many of the words have wings
Or run to type in small fleet herds
No question of retaining – what's the use!

Coming meanwhile to believe in you,
Fluent and native. Only read aloud
Do the words stay with me, through
Whose roots those flat clear vowels flow

To mirror, surfacing, the things they mean:
Blue heron, mountain, antelope, spruce, cloud.

2

Yesterday's flower, American Beauty
Crimson and sweet all night in the city,
Limp now, changed in import as in color,
Floats behind us in the tinkling cooler.

Yesterday also Robert Kennedy's
Train of refrigerated dignitaries
Last seen on TV burying Dr King
Wormed its way to Arlington Cemetary.

The beauty I mean to press fading
Between these lines is yours, and the misleading
Sweetness, leaves and portals of a body
Ajar, cool, nodding at the wheel already.

3
Dawn, the muted chirr and squeal – dream axle
Grinding your jaws? I mind for you
Prematurely.
In our roof are swallows,
Young ones breast to breast.

4
Next a high pool deep blue very hot
Illumination of the brimstone text
Beyond your windburned face panted and steamed
As did the spring left far below with death,

Its green rank to which we should return,
Two good men in high places out of breath
Less now than ant or tick the noon's cold bird
Lured to cast its ravenous milligram

Into the scale, and the small window steamed
Where I sat alone high blue
Taking stock of wing and wishbone stewed
At giddily low temperature –

Ice in the marrow of a star so pure
So beyond history, the eye-searing water
Onion or headline or your fine print drew
Dried in a wink, quick sleights of altitude.

5

Each day at dusk we roam the sage.
Heavenly repertory, bleakest rage

Bleeding to sour gleams, hard-edge jubilance,
All encompassed by one lariat glance.

The peaks turn baseless as the fear
That you will tell me what I live to hear.

Look, is all. The cabin. Look. The river.
Aspens glowing, site gloomed over.

Look. Out of thin air old gods (plume, hide, bead)
Appear to weigh your offerings of seed.

A leathery prospector god's pans fill
With foolsgold facets of my blackbird's trill.

Then all take umbrage in a blue
The silence positively ripples through.

6

From glade by river to a further day's
Thirst-crazed hilltop the abandoned cabin
Kept wandering like a mind with its few same
Obsessions, robin's nest and dish of rust,
Cracked pane dingily festooned,
Roof leaking sky, the same forty year old
Illustrated fictions sticking to its ribs

Where once again, the flask uncorked, two rooms
Are won back to this world,
Book by loaf a whole life dreams itself
From the foundation, from that withered rose
Mounted in antlers, up past the first morning
Glory's grasp of lightning rod,
Labor, cost, frostbite, bedazzlement,
Down to the last friend's guitar and stories,
Name called in sleep, fingers unclenching
In a long bath, its tepid amber inch
And dry bouquet – the future, gentlemen!

Tomorrow's cabin, who knows where, will seem
A shade sobered, abler to comprehend
How much, how little it takes to be thought worth
Crossing the threshold of, a place to dwell,
Will suffer once again the flashlight painless
Piercing of your dream, beam upon beam,
And its old boards before they turn to earth
Drink the mirage, the dreamer's volatile
Here all would have been well.

7
Sit then, draped in a sheet whose snowy folds
Darken in patches as when summer comes
And sun goes round and round the melting mountain.
Smiling debonair

You maybe wait for some not seen till now
Aspect of yours to blaze from the alembic
While one of mine in robe and slippers cries
Ah stay! Thou art so fair!

Or else are smiling not to wince recalling
Locks the grave sprang open. Blind, untrimmed,
Sheeted with cold, such rot and tangle must
In time be our affair.

But should you smile as those who doubt the novice
Hands they entrust their beautiful heads to,
I want to show you how the clumsiest love
Transfigures if you let it, if you dare.

There was a day when beauty, death, and love
Were coiled together in one crowning glory.
Shears in hand, we parted the dark waves . . .
Look at me, dear one. There.

8
Geode, the troll's melon
Rind of crystals velvet smoke meat blue
Formed far away under fantastic
Pressures, then cloven in two
By the taciturn rock shop man, twins now forever

Will they hunger for each other
When one goes north and one goes east?

I expect minerals never do.
Enough for them was a feast
Of flaws, the molten start and glacial sleep,
The parting kiss.

Still face to face in halfmoonlight
Sparkling comes easy to the Gemini.

Centimeters deep yawns the abyss.

9

Master of the ruined watercolor,
Citizen no less of the botched country
Where shots attain the eagle, and the grizzly
Dies for pressing people to his heart,

Truster, like me, of who (invoked by neither)
Hovered near the final evening's taper,
Held his breath to read his flickering nature
By our light, then left us in the dark,

Take these verses, call them today's flower,
Cluster a rained-in pupil might have scissored.
They too have suffered in the realm of hazard.
Sorry things all. Accepting them's the art.

Willowware Cup

Mass hysteria, wave after breaking wave
Blueblooded Cantonese upon these shores

Left the gene pool Lux-opaque and smoking
With dimestore mutants. One turned up today.

Plum in bloom, pagoda, blue birds, plume of willow –
Almost the replica of a prewar pattern –

The same boat bearing the gnat-sized lovers away,
The old bridge now bent double where her father signals

Feebly, as from flypaper, minding less and less.
Two smaller retainers with lanterns light him home.

Is that a scroll he carries? He must by now be immensely
Wise, and have given up earthly attachments, and all that.

Soon, of these May mornings, rising in mist, he will ask
Only to blend – like ink in flesh, blue anchor

Needled upon drunkenness while its destroyer
Full steam departs, the stigma throbbing, intricate –

Only to blend into a crazing texture.
You are far away. The leaves tell what they tell.

But this lone, chipped vessel, if it fills,
Fills for you with something warm and clear.

Around its inner horizon the old odd designs
Crowd as before, and seem to concentrate on you.

They represent, I fancy, a version of heaven
In its day more trouble to mend than to replace:

Steep roofs aslant, minutely tiled;
Tilted honeycombs, thunderhead blue.

Banks of a Stream Where Creatures Bathe

Through slits in the plantain leaf,
Celestial surge!
The fabulous old Goat
Extends nightlong

Ancien régime
Propositions. Stick with him
And you'll be wearing diamonds . . .
Barely relenting

You of the cool breast
Unclasp the rivière.
Facets reassembled
Pulse and scatter.

The courts of heaven
In sparkling shambles
Struggle against you
Like a shack on poles.

I can't compete.
Giving of my very
Self, I've seen you
Clouded by the gift.

You want diversions
Deeply pure, is that it?
Trust me. I keep trying
Not to break down.

I know the hoof
Imprinted on my clay,
His bulk and poise
Who drinks you, enters you;

And hold you close,
Too close to make the best
Of that recurrently
Real beast in you.

At dawn asleep
In fairness take these colors.
Do not sweep me
Downstream with the stars.

Under Mars

Cricket earphones fail us not
Here in the season of receptions

One prism drips ammonia still
Penknife-pearl-and-steel ripples

Paring nobody's orchard to the bone
Cut both ways the pond believes

And boulders' heavy sighs appear
Out of mown meadows and inside a head

Laid on the block you half erase
Chiefly to yourself antagonist

Our light fantastic fills the barn
Turning the Model A's stripped body gold

Turning it nightfall nothing space
Become emotion ball in full career

Frog-footmen croak those highnesses
Of empty sleeve and battle star

Who wither at a glance us gentlefolk
Though such as we have made them what they are

Yam

Rind and resurrection, hell and seed,
Fire-folia, hotbeds of a casserole
Divinely humble, it awaits your need.
Its message, taken in by you,

Deep reds obliterate. Be glad they do.
Go now by upward stages, fortified,
Where an imaginary line is being
Drawn past which you do not melt, you suffer

Pure form's utter discontent, white waste
And wintry grazing, flocks of white
But with no shepherd-sage, no flute, no phrases;
Parchment frozen, howling pricksong, mute

Periods that flash and stun –
Hit on the head, who brought you to this pass?
Valleys far below are spouting
Baby slogans and green gripes of spring,

Clogged pools, the floating yen . . .
You feel someone take leave, at once
Transfiguring, transfigured. A voice grunts
MATTER YOU MERELY DO I AM

Which lies on snow in dark ideogram
– Or as a later commentary words it,
One-night's-meat-another-morning's-mass-
Against-inhuman-odds-I-celebrate.

The Black Mesa

So much is parchment where I gloom,
Character still sharp enough to prick
Into the hide my igneous
Old spells and canticles of doom.
The things that shape a person! Peace.
Depth therapy in early stages crowned
One fuming anchorite with river stones.

Remember, though, how in *Thaïs*
The desert father falls for the land's lie –
That 'grande horizontale' (blown shawls
Shining and raveling to this day
Above erosions in her pot of rouge)
Whom any crossing cloud turns dim,
Ascetic, otherworldly, lost to him.

By way of you a thousand human
Frailties found in me their last refuge.
The turquoise lodged for good one night
In a crevice where the young blood drummed.
Discharge, salvo, sulfur ringed me round
Below the waist. I knew thirst. Dawns,
The viceroy's eagle glittered like a gnat.

Sieges like that come late and end
Soon. And we are friends now? Funny friends.
Glaringly over years you knit
A wild green lap robe I shake off in tears.
I steal past him who next reclaims you, keep
Our hushed appointments, grain by grain . . .
Dust of my dust, when will it all be plain?

Under Libra: Weights and Measures
for David McIntosh

The stones of spring,
Stale rolls or pellets rather, rounded
By a gorgon's fingers, swept to the floor,

Dragged south in crushing folds,
Long dirty tablecloth of ice,
Her feast ended, her intimates dispersed

Where certain curious formations
Dwindle in the red wind like ice in tea,
These stones, these poor scarred loaves

Lichen-crusted mould-gray or burnt orange
Stop doors and rest on manuscripts.
Backbreaking it was to haul them home.

Home. That winter's terrible storms,
Apartment shivering, whistling through its teeth,
Throb of a furnace fit to burst –

To go in the small hours from room to room
Stumbling onto their drugged stubborn sleep.

The heaviest dream
Gets told to the sunrise. The ditch
Hides its rapid and self-seeking nature

Beneath a blown glass simulacrum.
Mist and fire, tomorrow's opal
Defying gravity, inspiring it,

The sun will float across thin ice
To where two swans are dozing, swansdown quilts
Drawn over heads, feet tucked on top,

And snow be light as plumage upon theirs.
Paper windflowers like things possessed
Will dance upon Angel Ortiz

Leaving whose raw grave in the churchyard
The peacock, blue snake-neck zigzag
Through biscuit everlastings twice its height,

Will pass the shower window and not scream
Inward at a nude gone up in steam.

There then, his peacock
Past, the dreamer dries and gazes
Into the dormant crystal of himself,

A presence oval, vitrified –
That without warning thaws, trickles, and burns!
Frightened he looks away. He learns

To live whole days in another
Tense, avoid the bathroom scales or merely
Sing them. Wipe lather from his lip. Dress. Drive

Until the trees have leaves again
And the tanner's colors change to those of the mint,
Copper, silver, green

Engraved by summer's light, by spring's.
The riverbend's great horseshoe print
Where time turned round at last, drew rein,

Glints through a windshield blazing dust and wings,
Scum of the earth rebuffed upon the pane.

Warm afternoons
In his son's truck, Angel, both quick and dead,
Awaited judgment and suspended it.

His right side like a thing possessed
Danced, light birdclaw fast upon the guest.
The left had long let go – its tear

Oozed as from stone. It seemed
Both sides of the old character knew best.
In, out the unhinged doors

White coma'd spores were drifting, shining.
Flies lit, cudgeled quarter-carat wits,
Then washed their wings of him.

Blanca, too, who used to leap
Reeking of rain, licking his face like fire,
Lay back. Her coat caked red and speaking eyes

Clear as the baby's or the priest's
Wondered could he last another night.

For see, by dusk
A crescent jaw, a sudden frost of stubble
Yesterday's Gem will float across,

Enters the rear-view mirror. There was one
Direction only, after all?
How many more nights will that double-headed

Friend woven, wings outspread,
Into the dreamer's blanket keep him warm?
Here now's a little mesa set for two –

Over purple places, intimate
Twinklings, early stones, wide open spaces,
And soon on the horizon the "necklace of death"

Los Alamos' lights where wizards stay up late
(Stay in the car, forget the gate)
To save the world or end it, time will tell

– Mentioned for what it's worth in hopes
Of giving weight to – Brr! It's freezing!

Clay room. Firelight.
No measures taken, no words weighed –
As next morning, pen in hand, the whole

House sown by the prism on the sill
With arcs of spectral seed, a peacock's tail –
Or ten years from next morning, pen in hand,

Looking through saltwater, through flames,
Enkindlings of an absent *I* and *you*,
Live, spitting pronouns, sparks that flew

And were translated into windiest
Esperanto, zero tongue of powers
Diplomatic around 1 a.m.'s

Undripping centerpiece, the Swan . . .
Days were coming when the real thing
No longer shrugged a wing, dipping its mask

Where any surface thawed and burned.
One learned. The heavy stones of spring.
These autumn feathers. Learned.

Komboloi

the Greek "worry-beads"

Begin. Carnation underfoot, tea splashing stars
Onto this mottled slab, amber coherences,

Unmatched string of the habitué
Told and retold, rubbed lucid, quick with scenes . . .

That face – fire-slitted fur, whip fury, slate iced over!
Click. An early life. The warrior's

Came late, enchanted brief. Then, gem on brow
And far-eyed peregrine on wrist,

One life in profile brushed so fine
You felt no single stroke until the last of thousands.

All that while, the bed had flowed, divided,
Deepened and sung in sparkling attacks

None but whose woman brought her warm specific,
Her tongue unspeakable. Click. Taxis

Yoked together floors below were making
Summer hell. Yet from her pupil streamed

Radii such as gall the ferry's shadow
Plunging like my pen past shoals of shilly-shally

Into fathomless gentian. Or into
Some thinnest "shade" of blue

Juniper berries fallen on this far bank
Of now no river. Wingbeats echo where its ghost

Forks. Focus the half mile down
Upon snapped golds – if not a corn plantation

Then a small ill-strung harp which dead hands pluck
And pluck. No sound. No issue. The wheel

Founders in red rainwater, soul inchdeep in pain,
Charred spokesman of reflections grimly

Sanguine with siftings from the great
Cracked hourglass. Click. Will . . . ? Click.

Will second wind come even to the runners
Out of time? These beads – O marble counter – Done.

Strato in Plaster

στῆθος μάρμαρο καὶ καρδιὰ πατάτα

Out of the blue, in plaster from wrist to bicep
Somebody opens a beer, pretending to be
My friend Strato. Years or minutes – which? –
Have passed since we last looked upon each other.
He's in town for his sister's wedding
To this elderly thin-lipped sonofabitch
Who gets the house for dowry – enough to make
A brother break with the entire family.
Considering it, his eyes fairly cross
With self-importance. That, I recognize.

Here at hand is a postcard Chester sent
Of the Apollo at Olympia,
Its message *Strato as he used to be.*
Joy breeds in the beautiful blind gaze,
The marble mouth and breastbone. I look hard
At both the god and him. (He loves attention
Like gods and children, and he lifts his glass.)
Those extra kilos, that moustache,
Lies found out and letters left unanswered
Just won't do. It makes him burst out laughing,
Curiously happy, flecked with foam.

At present he is living far from home,
Builder by day and autocrat by dark,
Athenian among peasants. Fine Athenian
Whose wife learns acquiescence blow by blow.
That strikes a nerve. "I haven't married her!
Am I a fool to marry before thirty?
Who trusts a woman anyhow?
The nurse that set my elbow, filthy crone,
I cried out, it hurt so – but did she care?"
He goes on quickly, looking proud:

"I'm full of spite. Remember what you wrote
In answer to my asking for a loan?
I tore up your address – though you were right! –
Then sold the cufflinks and the black trenchcoat."

Now that he wants to go to El Dorado
His brother there has given up urging him.
"OK. I fuck his Virgin.
Bad son, bad father, and bad friend to you,
I might as well be a bad brother, too."
The little boy is three and "delicate"
But still "a devil, full of fight!"
My guest drinks up. Twin jewels unsold somehow,
His eyes are sparkling with delight.

Three winters, playing backgammon
At the café for stakes that pierce the heart,
One cigarette or dram of burning mud,
And never losing ("dice are in my blood") –
Marika sleeping, her cheeks ice,
Where oil smoke sickens and a chicken's cough
Wakes the child who dashes to the floor
Any red elixir *he* might pour –

Three winters. Trowels of frigid white
Choke the sugar-celled original
That once stayed warm all night with its own sun.
The god in him is a remembered one.
Inflexibility through which twinges shoot
Like stars, the fracture's too complex,
Too long unmended, for us to be friends.
I, he hazards, have made other friends.
The more reason, then, to part like friends.

Today at least a cloud of rice and petals
Aimed at others will envelop him.

Risen, he wonders – almost saying what.
I take his swollen hand in both of mine.
No syllable of certain grand tirades
One spent the worse part of a fall composing,
Merely that word in common use
Which means both *foolishness* and *self-abuse*
Coming to mind, I smile:
Was the break caused by too much malakía?
Strato's answer is a final burst
Of laughter: "No such luck!
One day like this the scaffold gave beneath me.
I felt no pain at first."

Up and Down

"The heart that leaps to the invitation
of sparkling appearances is the heart
that would itself perform as handsomely."
                John H. Finley, Jr., *Four Stages of Greek Thought*

I. *Snow King Chair Lift*

Prey swooped up, the iron love seat shudders
Onward into its acrophilic trance.
What folly has possessed us? Ambulance!
Give me your hand, try thinking of those others'

Unhurt return by twos from June's immense
Sunbeamed ark with such transfigured faces,
We sought admission on the shaky basis
That some good follows from experience

Of anything or leaving it behind,
As now, each urchin street and park sent sprawling
By the mountain's foot – why, this is fun, appalling
Bungalows, goodbye! dark frames of mind,

Whatever's settled into, comfort, despair,
Sin, expectation, apathy, the past,
Rigid interiors that will not outlast
Their decorator or their millionaire,

Groaning of board and bed of ruses, oh
I've had it up to here, fiftieth story
Glass maze, ice cube, daybreak's inflammatory
Montage subsiding into vertigo

Till, with their elevations all on file,
Joys, now demolished, that I used to live in,
This afternoon I swear halfway to heaven
None housed me – no, not style itself – in style.

Risen this far, your ex-materialist
Signs an impetuous long lease on views
Of several states and skies of several blues
Promptly dismantled by the mover mist

– What's going on? Loud ceiling shaken, brute
Maker of scenes in lightning spurt on spurt –
How did those others, how shall we avert
Illuminations that electrocute!

Except that suddenly the danger's gone.
Huge cloudscapes hang in the sun's antechamber.
Somebody takes our picture, calls a number.
We've done it. Reached the heights and quit our throne.

While knowing better, now, than to repeat
Our sole anabasis, unless in rhyme,
I love that funny snapshot from a time
When we still thought we were each other's meat.

The very great or very fatuous
Complicate the pinnacles they reach,
Plant banners, carve initials, end a speech,
"My fellow Texans, let us pray . . ." Not us.

You merely said you liked it in that chill
Lighthearted atmosphere (a crow for witness)
And I, that words profaned the driven whiteness
Of a new leaf. The rest was all downhill.

Au fond each summit is a cul-de-sac.
That day at least by not unprecedented
Foresight, a Cozy Cabin had been rented.
Before I led you to the next chair back

And made my crude but educated guess
At why the wind was laying hands on you
(Something I no longer think to do)
We gazed our little fills at boundlessness.

2. *The Emerald*

Hearing that on Sunday I would leave,
My mother asked if we might drive downtown.
Why certainly – off with my dressing gown!
The weather had turned fair. *We* were alive.

Only the gentle General she married
Late, for both an old way out of harm's,
Fought for breath, surrendered in her arms,
With military honors now lay buried.

That week the arcana of his medicine chest
Had been disposed of, and his clothes. Gold belt
Buckle and the letter from President Roosevelt
Went to an unknown grandchild in the West.

Downtown, his widow raised her parasol
Against the Lenten sun's not yet detectable
Malignant atomies which an electric needle
Unfreckles from her soft white skin each fall.

Hence too her chiffon scarf, pale violet,
And spangle-paste dark glasses. Each spring we number
The new dead. Above ground, who can remember
Her as she once was? Even I forget,

Fail to attend her, seem impervious . . .
Meanwhile we have made through a dense shimmy
Of parked cars burnished by the midday chamois
For Mutual Trust. Here cool gloom welcomes us,

And all, director, guard, quite palpably
Adore her. Spinster tellers one by one
Darting from cages, sniffling to meet her son,
Think of her having a son – ! She holds the key

Whereby palatial bronze gates shut like jaws
On our descent into this inmost vault.
The keeper bends his baldness to consult,
Brings a tin box painted mud-brown, withdraws.

She opens it. Security. Will. Deed.
Rummages further. Rustle of tissue, a sprung
Lid. Her face gone queerly lit, fair, young,
Like faces of our dear ones who have died.

No rhinestone now, no dilute amethyst,
But of the first water, linking star to pang,
Teardrop to fire, my father's kisses hang
In lipless concentration round her wrist.

Gray are these temple-drummers who once more
Would rouse her, girl-bride jeweled in his grave.
Instead, she next picks out a ring. "He gave
Me this when you were born. Here, take it for –

But bare. Baked crumbling meets
The children's hands. They've stumbled. It's nightfall.
"Come, Brüderlein,
The more living, the less truth.

On high till now obscured
Slow-stabbing instruments together
Sound their A.
Face the first music. Sleep."

Dreams About Clothes

for John and Anne Hollander

In some, the man they made
Penetrates the sunlit fitting room,
Once more deciding among bolts of dark.
The tailor kneels to take his measure.
Soon a finished suit will be laid out
By his valet, for him to change into.
Change of clothes? The very clothes of change!
Unchecked blazers women flutter round,
Green coverts, midnight blues . . .
My left hand a pincushion, I dispose,
Till morning, of whole closets full of clues.

What ought I in fact to do with them?
Give away suits worn six, eight times?
Take them to the shrink until they fit?
Have them mothproofed at least
(Arturo's Valet Service, one block East,
Picks up, delivers) – or just let them be,
Still holding sway above me, Harvard Law's
Loyal sons of 'oo hanging by claws
On their slow shuttle to the sea.

Sure enough, a waterfront
Glides into place on small, oiled waves.
Taverns are glittering and the heavens have cleared.
(Far inland lie the crossroads,
Oxcart overturned, graybeard
Lamented by his slaves.)
From whom did I inherit these shirtsleeves
And ancient, sexy jeans?
Fingers of a woman I am with

Tease through holes made by the myth.
Bad music starts in 6/8 time.
I order drinks and dinners. I'm
Being taken, her smile means
Once more to the cleaners.

Sleeping clean through those August afternoons
Whose Prospero, on shuttles quick as play,
Was weaving rainy spells –
Warp of physics, woof of whim;
Feeling him under some new pressure thunder
Forth in loud black surges to outsweat
Until the lightning twinkling of an eye
Dissolved his corporation,
The tempest used to be my cup of tea.
(Come in, Mme de Garments called,
You'll be soaked to the skin! I never woke.)
Relief poured through me shining wet,
Lining of purest silver.

But now, his baby face unlined and bald,
The old-clothes man comes down the street,
Singing the little song he sings.
His overcoat is all humped up in back
To hide his powerful wings.
Snow melts at the touch of his bare feet.
He passes me unseeing, yet how much
Of mine's already in his sack!

Tell me something, Art.
You know what it's like
Awake in your dry hell
Of volatile synthetic solvents.
Won't you help us brave the elements

Once more, of terror, anger, love?
Seeing there's no end to wear and tear
Upon the lawless heart,
Won't you as well forgive
Whoever settles for the immaterial?
Don't you care how we live?

Flèche d'Or

Windowglass, warmed plush, a sneeze
Deflected by the miracle
Into euphoria's
Authoritative gliding forth,
The riddle of the rails
Vitally unmoved in flight
However fast
I run racing that arrow
Lodged in my brain
Down the board platform beyond hurt or hope
Once more, once more
My life ended, having not,
Veils lifted, words from the page
Come to my senses
Eased of that last arrivederci deep
In book or view, my own
Fleet profile calmer catapulted due
North a pane floats off, desire sinks
Red upon piercing stubble – "Traveler,
Turn back!" the tracks
Outcry, din flash fade, done,
Over forever, done I say, now yet
Might somebody
Seeing it all (for once not I or I)
Judge us wisely in whose heart of
Hearts the parallels
Meet and nothing lasts and nothing ends.

Days of 1971

Fallen from the clouds, well-met.
This way to the limousine.
How are things? Don't tell me yet!
Have a Gauloise first, I mean.

Matches now, did I forget –
With a flourish and no word
Out came the sentry-silhouette
Black against a big, flame-feathered bird,

Emblem of your "new" regime
Held, for its repressive ways,
In pretty general disesteem

Which to share just then was hard,
Borne up so far on a strategic blaze
Struck by you, and quite off guard.

In Paris you remark each small
Caged creature, marmoset, bat, newt, for sale;
Also the sparkling gutters, and the smelly
Seine this afternoon when we embark.

And the Bateau Mouche is spoiled by a party of cripples.
Look at what's left of that young fellow strapped
Into his wheelchair. How you pity him!
The city ripples, your eyes sicken and swim.

The boy includes you in his sightseeing,
Nodding sociably as if who of us
Here below were more than half a man.

64

There goes the Louvre, its Egyptian wing
Dense with basalt limbs and heads to use
Only as one's imagination can.

Can-can from last night's *Orphée aux Enfers*
Since daybreak you've been whistling till I wince.
Well, you were a handsome devil once.
Take the wheel. You're still a fair chauffeur.

Our trip. I'd pictured it another way –
Asthmatic pilgrim and his "nun of speed,"
In either mind a music spun of need . . .
That last turnoff went to Illiers.

Proust's Law (are you listening?) is twofold:
(a) What least thing our self-love longs for most
Others instinctively withhold;

(b) Only when time has slain desire
Is his wish granted to a smiling ghost
Neither harmed nor warmed, now, by the fire.

Stephen in the Pyrenees – our first
Real stop. You promptly got a stomachache.
Days of groans and grimaces interspersed
With marathon slumbers. Evenings, you'd wake

And stagger forth to find us talking. Not
Still about poetry! Alas . . .
So bottles were produced, and something hot.
The jokes you told translated, more or less.

Predictably departure cured you. Stephen
Investing me with a Basque walking stick,
"How much further, James, will you be driven?"

He didn't ask. He stood there, thin, pale, kind
As candlelight. Ah, what if *I* took sick?
You raced the motor, having read my mind.

Sucked by haste into the car,
Pressing his frantic buzzer, Bee!
Suppose he stings – why such hilarity?
These things occur.

Get rid of him at once
While we can! His wrath
Is almost human, the windshield's warpath
Dins with a song and dance

In one respect unlike our own:
Readily let out into the open.
There. Good creature, also he had known
The cost of self-as-weapon;

Venom unspent, barb idle, knows
Where they lead now – thyme, lavender, musk-rose,

Toulouse, Toulon, the border. Driven?
At ease, rather among fleeting scenes.
The O L I V E T T I signs
Whizz by, and azure Lombardy is given

Back, as the Virgin of Officialdom
Severely draped twists on her throne to peek
At the forbidden crags of kingdom come
Before resuming her deft hunt and peck.

One V sticks. Venice. Its vertiginous pastry
Maze we scurry through like mice and will
Never see the likes of in our lives.

It is too pink, white, stale to taste,
Crumbling in the gleam of slimy knives.
Have your cake and eat it? Take the wheel.

Wait – now where are we? Who is everyone?
Well, that's a Princess, that's the butler . . . no,
Probably by now the butler's son.
We were stopping till tomorrow with Umberto

Among trompe l'oeil, old volumes, photographs
Of faded people wearing crowns and stars.
Welcome to the Time Machine, he laughed
Leaning on us both up its cold stairs.

At table the others recalled phrases from
Homer and Sappho, and you seemed to brighten.
Your sheets would entertain the 'priest' that night
(Dish of embers in a wooden frame)

And eyes glaze on the bedside book, remote
But near, pristine but mildewed, which I wrote.

Take the wheel. San Zeno will survive
Whether or not visited.
Power is knowledge in your head.
(Sorry, I must have been thinking aloud. Drive, drive.)

Time and again the novel I began
Took aim at that unwritten part
In which the hero, named Sebastian,
Came to his senses through a work of art.

O book of hours, those last
Illuminated castles built
In air, O chariot-motif

Bearing down a margin good as gilt
Past fields of ever purer leaf
Its burning rubric, to get nowhere fast . . .

The road stopped where a Greek mountain fell
Early that week. Backed-up cars glared in the dusk.
Night fell next, and still five stupid slack-
Jawed ferries hadn't got their fill of us.

Tempers shortened. One self-righteous truck
Knocked the shit out of a eucalyptus
Whose whitewashed trunk lay twitching brokenly –
Nijinsky in *Petrouchka* – on the quai.

Later, past caring, packed like sheep,
Some may have felt the breathless lounge redeemed
By a transistor singing to the doomed

At last in their own tongue. You fell asleep
Life-sentenced to the honey-cell of song,
Harsh melisma, torturous diphthong.

Strato, each year's poem
Says goodbye to you.
Again, though, we've come through
Without losing temper or face.

If care rumpled your face
The other day in Rome,
Tonight just dump my suitcase
Inside the door and make a dash for home

While I unpack what we saw made
At Murano, and you gave to me –
Two ounces of white heat
Twirled and tweezered into shape,

Ecco! another fanciful
Little horse, still blushing, set to cool.

The Victor Dog

for Elizabeth Bishop

Bix to Buxtehude to Boulez,
The little white dog on the Victor label
Listens long and hard as he is able.
It's all in a day's work, whatever plays.

From judgment, it would seem, he has refrained.
He even listens earnestly to Bloch,
Then builds a church upon our acid rock.
He's man's – no – he's the Leiermann's best friend,

Or would be if hearing and listening were the same.
Does he hear? I fancy he rather smells
Those lemon-gold arpeggios in Ravel's
'Les jets d'eau du palais de ceux qui s'aiment.'

He ponders the Schumann Concerto's tall willow hit
By lightning, and stays put. When he surmises
Through one of Bach's eternal boxwood mazes
The oboe pungent as a bitch in heat,

Or when the calypso decants its raw bay rum
Or the moon in *Wozzeck* reddens ripe for murder,
He doesn't sneeze or howl; just listens harder.
Adamant needles bear down on him from

Whirling of outer space, too black, too near –
But he was taught as a puppy not to flinch,
Much less to imitate his bête noire Blanche
Who barked, fat foolish creature, at King Lear.

Still others fought in the road's filth over Jezebel,
Slavered on hearths of horned and pelted barons.
His forebears lacked, to say the least, forbearance.
Can nature change in him? Nothing's impossible.

The last chord fades. The night is cold and fine.
His master's voice rasps through the grooves' bare groves.
Obediently, in silence like the grave's
He sleeps there on the still-warm gramophone

Only to dream he is at the première of a Handel
Opera long thought lost – *Il Cane Minore*.
Its allegorical subject is his story!
A little dog revolving round a spindle

Gives rise to harmonies beyond belief,
A cast of stars. . . . Is there in Victor's heart
No honey for the vanquished? Art is art.
The life it asks of us is a dog's life.

Syrinx

Bug, flower, bird on slipware fired and fluted,
The summer day breaks everywhere at once.

Worn is the green of things that have known dawns
Before this, and the darkness before them.

Among the wreckage, bent in Christian weeds,
Illiterate – X my mark – I tremble, still

A thinking reed. Who puts his mouth to me
Draws out the scale of love and dread –

O ramify, sole antidote! Foxglove
Each year, cloud, hornet, fatal growths

Proliferating by metastasis
Rooted their total in the gliding stream.

Some formula not relevant any more
To flower children might express it yet

Like $\sqrt{\left(\dfrac{x}{y}\right)^n} = \mathrm{I}$

– Or equals zero, one forgets –

The y standing for you, dear friend, at least
Until that hour he reaches for me, then

Leaves me cold, the great god Pain,
Letting me slide back into my scarred case

Whose silvery breath-tarnished tones
No longer rivet bone and star in place

Or keep from shriveling, leather round a stone,
The sunbather's precocious apricot

Or stop the four winds racing overhead
                    Nought
          Waste   Eased
                    Sought

James Merrill

James Merrill was born in New York City and now
lives in Stonington, Connecticut. He is the author
of five other books of poems, one of which, *Nights
and Days,* received the National Book Award in
Poetry for 1967. He has also written two novels, *The
(Diblos) Notebook* (1965) and *The Seraglio* (1957), and
two plays, *The Immortal Husband* (first produced in
1955 and published in Playbook the following year)
and, in one act, *The Bait,* published in Artist's
Theatre (1960).